Following Rules

by Robin Nelson

first step nonfiction

Lerner Publications Company · Minneapolis

I follow **rules.**

Rules keep us safe.

Rules make things fair.

Rules help us get along.

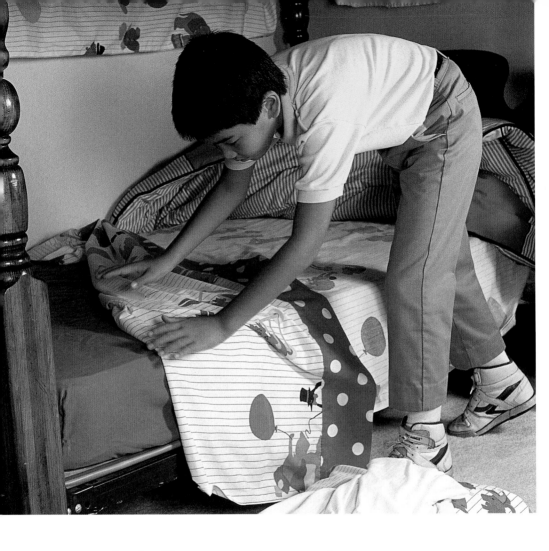

I follow rules at home.

I clean my room.

I throw balls outside.

I help with **chores.**

I follow rules at school.

I walk in the halls.

I raise my hand.

I use a quiet voice.

I follow rules in my **community.**

I do not **litter.**

I wait to **cross** the street.

I follow rules every day.

How can you follow rules at home?

- Follow rules while playing a game.

- Tell the truth.

- Wash your hands before dinner.

- Finish your homework before playing.

- Listen to adults you live with.

How can you follow rules at school?

- Do not cheat during tests.

- Be respectful of others.

- Wait for your turn.

- Follow directions.

- Include everyone.

Glossary

 chores – tasks that need to be done

 community – the area where a group of people live

 cross – to go to the other side

 litter – to leave trash around

 rules – words that tell how to behave

Index

The photographs in this book are reproduced through the courtesy of: © Jacques M. Chenet/ CORBIS, front cover; © Connie Summers, pp. 2, 15, 22 (second from bottom); © Betty Crowell, pp. 3, 17, 22 (bottom); © Todd Strand/Independent Picture Service, pp. 4, 5, 10, 12, 13; © Steven Ferry, p. 6; © Geri Engberg, p. 7; © Brand-X Pictures, p. 8; © Rich Pomerantz, pp. 9, 22 (top); © Stockbyte, p. 11; PhotoDisc, pp. 14, 22 (second from top); © Jack McConnell, pp. 16, 22 (middle).

Illustrations on pages 19 and 21 by Tim Seeley.

Lerner Publications Company
A division of Lerner Publishing Group
241 First Avenue North
Minneapolis, MN 55401 U.S.A.

Website address: www.lernerbooks.com

Library of Congress Cataloging-in-Publication Data

Nelson, Robin, 1971–
        Following rules / by Robin Nelson.
            p.   cm. — (First step nonfiction)
        Includes index.
        Summary: An introduction to following rules at school, at home, and in the community, with specific examples of how to follow the rules at home and at school.
        ISBN: 0–8225–1284–X (lib. bdg. : alk. paper)
        1. Children—Conduct of life—Juvenile literature. 2. Obedience—Juvenile literature.
    [1. Obedience. 2. Conduct of life.] I. Title. II. Series.
    BJ1631 .N35 2003
    170'.83'4—dc21   2002000601

Manufactured in the United States of America
3 4 5 6 7 8 – DP – 10 09 08 07 06 05